CW00343415

Best wishes

Mick O'...

22nd June

2012

The Kiss

Ulick O'Connor

*New and Selected Poems
and Translations*

salmonpoetry

Published in 2008 by
Salmon Poetry Ltd.,
Cliffs of Moher, County Clare, Ireland
Website: www.salmonpoetry.com
Email: info@salmonpoetry.com

ISBN 978-1-903392-97-3

Cover artwork: Portrait of Ulick O'Connor by Patrick O'Connor, 1958,
(photographed by David Conachy)

Cover design & typesetting: Siobhán Hutson

Acknowledgments

These poems are selected from four books of verse and a book of verse plays: *Lifestyles* (1973 Hamish Hamilton) and Dolmen Press, *All Things Counter* (1986 The Dedalus Press), *One is Animate* (1990 Beaver Row Press), *Poems of the Damned* (1995 Wolfhound Press) and *Three Noh Plays* (1980 Wolfhound Press), *Les Fleurs du Mal, Translations from Charles Baudelaire* (1995 Wolfhound Press). Additional poems were published in journals between 1980-2006.

Special thanks to Joseph Woods of Poetry Ireland and to Anna Harrison.

Contents

EIGHTEEN POEMS BY CHARLES BAUDELAIRE from
Les Fleurs du Mal translated by Ulick O'Connor

Foreword

Ulick O'Connor retains the vivid sense of how Ireland once was, and these supremely splendid heartfelt selected poems do in their significant way not only reflect his love and his understanding for his country but they also contribute to upholding Ireland's continued literary importance.

Wonderfully written by one of Ireland's outstanding athletes, a pole-vaulting champion no less, who proves also to be a master poet.

Long may he reign.

J P DONLEAVY
27th June 2008

The Kiss

She said to me
"Kiss me specially",
And with her lips on mine
Traced a design
To show the way
Bees on a drowsy day
Suck honey from fuchsia.
How could I be so sure
That the artificer who spun
The golden honeycomb
For her at Erice,
The goddess in exile,
Could ever have gleaned
What I found
When I leaned
To that command.

(*One is Animate*, 1990)

NOTE: Daedalus, the legendary Greek smith, came in springtime to Erice to give thanks for his escape from King Minos on the island of Crete. He had designed wings which enabled him to fly to Sicily and proceed to Erice where Pilgrims would come with presents to honour Aphrodite. In this way Daedalus offered the goddess in thanksgiving a unique gift of a golden honeycomb so well fashioned that it was indistinguishable from a real one. Today near Pantálica in Sicily a great honeycomb hangs in the caves golden in the sun, and refreshed constantly by the resonant flight of bees, who continually arrive to increase the shine of the glinting web.

Requiem For A Nanny

(Ann Bell died August 1984)

I

I saw from the water bus,
Like a dot on the piazza,
An old lady emerge
From the gloom of San Giorgio.

It reminded me of you
Who fifty years before
Taught me the Stations of the Cross
In our church at Rathgar.

Taught me to "salute"
Priest – and parson too –
For you were from Tyrone
Where that was the thing to do.
Yes, I was brought up well
By Nanny, Ann Bell.

II

For you the Church of the Three Patrons
Was a temple of delight,
Tented by that soaring roof
You made your own rite.

Loosed your mind from time to time
To join in the liturgy's swell,
The delicious strangeness of the Latin,
Accept the discipline of the bell.

When in your ninetieth year
I took a chance and walked you down
(It didn't take a feather out of you
You wanted to walk home on your own),

We went round the familiar altars,
Murmured to the Little Flower,
Touched the feet of St. Anthony,
Knelt for the Holy Hour.

It seemed like before, except
That beside you I was an empty shell,
Not feeling in that silent nave
The peace that enveloped you like a spell.

III

On your way out
I glanced at the organ loft
Where Joyce's father met his wife
And thought of that devious poet,

But was careful not to mention it,
Even in a passing phrase,
For I knew you thought him responsible
For most of my wayward ways.

(*All Things Counter*, 1986)

Homage to Sean MacBride

(Died 16th July 1988)

(Winner of Nobel Prize for Peace and Lenin Peace Prize)

Always I remember you in that house
Standing at the door to welcome us,
The touch of the seigneur in your stance,
But the warmth of the chieftain in your glance.
Then, noticing as the night wore on [1]
How her presence filled the room
Like the scent of a faint perfume
That lingers after the beloved has gone.

In your talk legends were begotten –
"W.B. taught me English; Ezra, Latin".
And the mind recalled what the poet had said –
"That straight back and arrogant head".
In this forge she shaped what she held dear
To free Ireland and release her sex
From man-made laws, this was her text.
Constance [2], Hannah [3], Charlotte [4] all worked here.

You had the comprehension without which
There is no making sense of this crazy pitch,
How someone bred from high intent and creed
May tip the scales, unleash a fearful deed.
Yet had not that cast of mind prevailed,
Slouched like a dolt beside the fire
Savouring his anger like desire,
Would have let the pot simmer till it boiled.

In that book-lined room I watched many a night
You finger out a clause, begin the fight
To save some man; with dawn the firelight danced
On those high cheekbones, and the mind had chanced
On that fantastic knight; could one man find
So much to joust against and win?
Armoured with argument you went in,
Your lance the lightning flourish of the mind.

Now at your funeral a Cardinal talks,
Yeats' verses clamour through the vaults,
Lenin too, is named. So much has changed
Through you. At your grave the Army ranged
To present arms. The same, which from your cell
Took Rory to the firing squad.[5]
But that, too, has been turned to good,
More accomplished by a guiding will.

Through the streets the funeral takes its way,
An old woman grasps me by the hand to say –
"You could listen to her all night". That face
Again intrudes upon our space,
You and she in that great tale revealed,
Which he thought alone worthy of theme,
The people's book which holds the dream
When all that's left of Tara is a field.

(*One is Animate*, 1990)

NOTES:
[1] Sean MacBride was the son of the beautiful and aristocratic
Maud Gonne whom Yeats wrote many well known love
poems to. She was a fighter for women's rights and Irish
Nationalism and was adored by the Irish working classes.

[2] Constance Markievicz, (née Gore-Booth), revolutionary. Condemned to death but reprieved for her part in the Rebellion of 1916. The subject of one of Yeats' finest poems. Elected to Westminster in 1918, Constance Markievicz was the first woman Member of Parliament.

[3] Hannah Sheehy Skeffington, along with Maud Gonne and Constance Markievicz was prominent in the struggle for Women's Rights and a supporter of the Suffragette Movement.

[4] Charlotte Despard, one of the founding members of the Suffragette Movement in England and a sister of Lord French, Commander-in-Chief of the British Forces in Ireland. Charlotte Despard devoted the later years of her life to working for Ireland and lived with Maud Gonne in Roebuck House.

[5] In the Civil War in 1922 Sean MacBride was on the Anti-Treaty side which opposed the new Irish Free State Army. He was arrested and shared a cell with one of the leaders of the Anti-Treaty forces Rory O'Connor who on 8th December, 1922 was taken from the cell and executed by an Army firing squad as a reprisal.

Forty Shades

Let us calumniate green:
It weakens the will in us,
A most unholy sheen
Inducing paralysis.

Midsummer meadows, afloat
In lush heat, throw a blue glow
But beneath lurks the greencoat
Inertia, cop out, no go.

Close the eyes? Yes! Ask still
Is this the right emphasis?
Is darkness negotiable
Without the paralysis.

(*One Is Animate*, 1990)

Autumn Fire

Falling
leaf.
Where is the
grief.

When trees burst
out
in this brave
shout.

This is Spring's
breath
which cowards call
Death.

(2006)

Autumn Scare

It is heartening, though the leaves brown,
To see the pert blackberry look down
Tart to the tongue with bright gleam.
But today fear crackled off the crop,
Time has telescoped to make it seem
A week since Fall last fired the trees' top.

(2006)

The Piper's Club

The leaping finger tightens on the string.
Bow slips sideways in a sudden swoop;
The fiddler's found his air; with head on swing,
His glazed eyes ignore the captive group.

But oh! my knuckles whiten at my plight.
What silken word can match the fiddler's fling
Who saw a blackbird in a gap of light
And trapped its sweetness on a tightened string?

(*Life Styles*, 1973)

Awakening

Your eyes shone as if you'd seen
The first spring quiver into being,
That morning when I brushed your lips
To win you back from sleep's eclipse.
Had we slipped our moorings in a race
Beyond the edge to another place?
But the oars were set; you won't deny this
We touched lands fabled as Atlantis.

(1986)

Two Deaths

I

Loosed limbs dropped,
Flaked out from the zenith,
Not on an Aegean isle
But a crumpled bedsheet.
La petite mort
Before
We become ourselves once more.

II

You knew you'd had it
From the look in her eye;
You didn't exist any more,
She was wired into another guy.
Dames can't get it on again,
For them there is no Spring
Once *l'amour* is on the wane,
It's curtains, finito, the real thing.

(*One Is Animate*, 1990)

One Up

It wasn't because
She was half aristocrat,
She was just French
And that was that.
That marble brow
And curved mouth
Could never know
The centuries of drought
Which plagued my kin
Till they ate agony
Swallowed hatred, made songs spin
From melancholy.
But one day
I caught her on the hop
Made her laugh
As if she would never stop,
Shattered her fine face
Until she knew
None of her fancy French boys
Could do what I could do
Because they lacked, you see,
Centuries of agony.

(*Life Styles*, 1973)

The Stare

(To a cat named Sir Alfred)

From behind your eyes pyramids gleam
As if you'd glimpsed an elementary plan
Spinning till it slowly stopped, to seem
An image from a world beyond our span.

You seemed indifferent to the russet glow
Radiating from that splendid pelt
As if to say "There are other things you know
More important and more deeply felt."

And oh! The compliment I one time got
When I came one night to Derrybawn
And found you on the driveway in your special spot
To greet me as I crossed the moonlit lawn.

Eyeball to eyeball we explored terrains
Yours the cat kingdom, mine what man endures.
Your image in my inward eye remains
Dear Alfie, do I still survive in yours?

(1991)

Princess – 5th September, 1997

They said it was the funeral of a fair young lass
Whom everyone loved, and wept to see it pass.
But he lay in the gutter with a needle in his arm
And was unable to join in the general alarm.

Why are they crying Mummy, wailing like the wind
Is it because some great one, greviously has sinned?
No my little lambkin we must keep it to ourselves
The people who are crying there are crying for themselves.

Vampire

The saddest thing she ever said
Was "Send me a photo of the Left Bank",
She who scarcely ever had been out of home.
Arklow was the limit of her think tank –
Slim, lovely lackadaisical Liffey Queen.
Her mother had her tentacles in her,
Used her as a buffer against da,
Till in the end there was only one winner.
She never saw the Left Bank
Or Arklow again with its chatter.
For she died at thirty from an undiagnosed disease,
And that was the end of the matter
Except that her mother made out on her sweeney,
The life and soul of an old folks' home in Raheny.

(*All Things Counter*, 1986)

Marcel

(Á la Recherche du Temps Perdu, 1916-1918)

From the Ritz, where he had dined
En celibitaire, to a room cork-lined
To soak up sound – was Marcel's routine
Except once a week to change the scene
He would stroll to his pet brothel, where, eye glued
To spy-hole, he would watch men in the nude,
His *plat du jour*, a *poilu* paid,
(Fresh from the Front and his killing trade)
To prance round naked and skewer a rat,
This is what Marcel was playing at
While others played the game of Death
(It's hard to talk of them in the same breath).
But his business was to ferret out
Marcel: not care who else was up the spout.
He could claim the sheafs beside his bed
Would live, when millions more were dead.

(One Is Animate, 1990)

From Prison

After Verlaine

The sky above the roof is
So blue, so calm,
The tree above the roof
Cradles it's palm.

A bell one sees in the sky
Makes music faint,
A bird calls out nearby
Its sweet complaint.

God, O God, out there is life,
Simple and apart,
How peaceful that murmur comes
From the village heart.

What have you done, oh you who pass
In the midst of tears?
Say, passerby, what have you done
With the vanished years?

Translated by Ulick O'Connor
(*All Things Counter*, 1986)

Ernesto Lynch–Guevara

(1928-1967)

The trouble with revolutions
Is that they usually end up
With the same solutions
As the crowd they've sent up.

But you, when the job was done
And spoils for the taking,
Went off to the next one
Without waiting.

Like a poet, who won't hear
An old poem played back,
You got yourself in the clear,
Cut a new track.

It never made the charts
But it's going to be around
When the next one starts
And they need a new sound.

(One is Animate, 1990)

Auschwitz

They fumed for weeks but could not steer
Oswiecem into the calm of their own sound,
The Slav syllable defied the Teuton ear,
Nothing to match it could be found.
Then one day listening with half-cocked ear,
In half disgust to close a gap,
The Boss spat out "Auschwitz" to the clerk
Who dutifully inscribed it on the map
A fixture for the victor

Later from these lush fields the camps sprang,
The chambers with their interminable dead,
Auschwitz [1] now seemed impeccably bred,
As hiss of gas and oven's clang
Made that first haphazard conclusion
A nifty logo for the final solution [2]

But to take the matter to another phase
If the Boss had been of scholarly bent
And made enquiries in that ancient space
As to what Oswiecem actually meant
And discovered it came out as "Blessed Place"
Would the news have brought elation to his face.
A divine endorsement for that appalling claim
That what was done was enacted in His Name.

(*One is Animate*, 1990)

NOTES:

[1] Auschwitz is a non-word which the Nazis cobbled together to represent the Polish name Oswiecem. *The Moravian Dictionary* (1911) translates Os-Wiecem as "Blessed Place".

[2] "We want to prevent our Germany from suffering, as Another did, the death upon the Cross."
Adolf Hitler, Munich 20th April 1923.

Louis MacNeice

(1907-1963)

Even the Antrim hills
he glimpsed through a fog of gasometer bigotry;
and when he tramped Connemara (his father's land)
his heart leaped to thrill of fife and drum,
to dull the lure of Papish hills.
Rather than accept ship or linen trade
He chose London pub,
Ariel piping aloft,
and deraciné
ground out a testament.
I saw him in his last year
at some Joyce affair outside the Tower,
looking, granite-faced, away from the sea,
feeling the tug of Ireland.

(Life Styles, 1973)

For Gerard Murphy

Poet and Scholar (1901-1958)

My ear Englished, I might never have found
Beneath the halting cadence and hoarse ring
Of our Irish verse, that sunken music,
If one day you had not brought
Before the mind a line of O'Rahilly's
And as you teased the words out,
Caressing their assonances
Like a lover repeating endearments,
I wanted somehow to find the key
To unlock what was imprisoned in me.

(*One Is Animate*, 1990)

The Coolin
(The fair-haired one)

from the Irish

Have you seen the Coolin abroad on the road there,
Her dainty shoes twinkling in the dewy morning air,
There's many a greeneyed lad, and to wed her is his dream,
But he wouldn't get my treasure so easy as it would seem.

My joy, when she's alone in the morning to behold her,
Twining gold tresses tumbling on her shoulder.
The rose-red and honey-sweet of her cheeks enhance her,
To have her for his sweetheart is the wish of every chancer.

Have you seen my bright love at the edge of the sea,
Her hair, with gold ringed fingers arranging gracefully.
It was Power, the master of the ship, who swore
That he would rather she'd be his, than that Ireland would
    be divided no more.

(1979)

NOTE: Of the melody in this Irish song Beethoven remarked:
'I would have been glad indeed to have composed such a work'.

Oscar Wilde

(from the Irish of Brendan Behan)

After all the wit
In a sudden fit
Of fear, he skipped it.
Stretched in the twilight
That body once lively
Dumb in the darkness
In a cold empty room.
Quiet, but for candles
Blazing beside him,
His elegant form
and firm gaze exhausted.
With a spiteful concierge
Impatient at waiting
For a foreign waster
Who left without paying
The ten per cent service.
Exiled now from Flore
To sanctity's desert
The young prince of Sin
Broken and withered.
Lust left behind him
Gem without lustre
No pernod for a stiffner
But cold holy water
The young king of Beauty
Narcissus broken.
But the pure star of Mary
As a gleam on the ocean.

ENVOI
Sweet is the way of the sinner,
Sad, death without God's praise.
My life on you Oscar boy,
Yourself had it both ways.

(*Life Styles*, 1973)

A Jackeen Says Goodbye to the Blaskets

(from the Irish of Brendan Behan)

The great sea under the setting sun gleams like a glass,
Not a sail in sight, no living person to see it pass
Save the last golden eagle, hung on the edge of the world,
Over the lonely Blasket resting, his wings unfurled.

Yes, the sun's at rest now and shadows thicken the light,
A rising moon gleams coldly through the night,
Stretching thin fingers down the quivering air,
On desolate, deserted dwellings, pitifully bare.

Silent save for birds' wings clipping the foam,
Heads on breast, they rest content, grateful to be home.
The wind lifts lightly, setting the half-door aslope,
On a famished hearth without heat, without protection,
    without hope.

(Life Styles, 1973)

NOTE: Jackeen – The Irish countryman's name for a Dubliner.
The last inhabitants left the Blasket Islands in 1948.

For Francis Stuart After being Named "Wise Man" October 1996

How odd indeed they should have chosen you
Who always chose unwisely with intent.
Who favoured failure so you could pursue
That adventure which misadventure sent.

And when I asked what talisman it was
That kept you buoyant on the darkening flood
"Patience" you murmured after a long pause.
And your smile said more than any wise man could.

(1996)

NOTE: Aosdána (the Irish Academy for writers, musicians and artists) elected Francis Stuart Saoi in 1996. Saoi means in Gaelic "Wise Man".

Carrion Comfort

I often sensed in the crow's caw
Something akin to the death rattle,
But now, as surgeons hurried to and fro
Arming their team for battle,
I watched a black blanket of crows
Shaken out from the trees' sheet,
As in a great clatter of noise they rose,
I thought I never heard anything so sweet.

(*One Is Animate*, 1990)

Astronaut

(July 20, 1969)

For too long we had watched them fade, the flickering lights
That led along corridors to an empty palace,
Till in the end, even the monuments of nature seemed
Part of a conspiracy of universal malice.

Night seemed unassailable with its endless galaxies,
The last gateway through which we could arrange an exit,
But that silence, which should have greeted the first
    tremulous footfall,
Is shattered now by the measured murmur of the heart beat.

(All Things Counter, 1986)

Immortality

Long John Coffey held an elegant cue,
But a job would turn down with a passion:
Just click, click, click, the balls that he sank,
In such exceptional fashion.
At one o'clock sharp he went back home,
Where mother had his dinner on the table.
Then back again to the saloon at three,
To sink them as only he was able.
At six o'clock he rigidly stopped,
For mother was strict about mealtime:
He attended devotions and never missed Mass,
Took her for walks in his free time.
I saw him the other day, tall, upright, spruce,
Eighty, though you'd never have thought it,
Preserved in the amber of a mother's care
Though by now she must certainly have bought it;
But coffined or not she is alive and true
In Long John Coffey who held an elegant cue.

(*All Things Counter*, 1986)

Vatican Two

There was a miraculous melody from that chamber,
The birds sang there all day
And in the square outside
Hundreds gathered to listen.
Then one day he said,
"I will let all the birds out"
And opened the window
And they flew to the four corners of the earth.
They called him afterwards, liberator,
Some even called him a saint.
But without the singing birds
The chamber soon fell into decay
And became in the end
A haunt for tourists.

(*All Things Counter*, 1986)

Foiled

I am cheesed off with memory
Each year I cross the Atlantic
And I visit the same places.
It makes me absolutely frantic,
My eye tells me it's the same,
Judas mind agrees with the eye,
But I know it's not the same.
Something does die,
It is quite infuriating to sit
At this table in New York, damned,
Because I feel it more alive in my mind
Than when I touch it with my hand.

(*Life Styles*, 1973)

Thoughts on the Four Hundredth Anniversary of the Battle of Kinsale

Wales today is plain
Where they crown a prince,
Tinsel and gown convince
Mob, as in Henry's reign.
From Kinsale Head
Ireland sends no ill wish
That's their dish
We chose different bread.
Here our hopes toppled
The last gun boomed
The Gael was doomed
Soon drained to a trickle.
Unlike fickle
Scot or Welsh
We didn't welsh.
How was it priced
What secret lurked
In the blood?
Our saviour
The bright body of Christ
Under a thin wafer.
That worked.

(*Life Styles*, 1973)

NOTE: At the Battle of Kinsale in 1601 Hugh O'Neill, Earl of Tyrone, was defeated by the English Army under Lord Mountjoy, and the hopes of Gaelic Ireland perished.

Messages

On 10th August 1981 the first of ten hunger strikers died at
Long Kesh internment camp, Antrim, in pursuit of political
status and the right to wear their own clothes.

Thinking of Apollo who went down among the swineherds
And of One who elected to be born in a stable,
I thought of those in Belfast who traced excrement on
    their cell walls
To send the world a message along the spirit's cable.

Then the final throw, the refusal of sap to the body,
The mind roaring along swerved avenues of agony,
Bishops shanghaied to tell them their soul was in danger,
As the jailers discovered the value of Catholic theology.

That they should let you die rather than wear your own jacket
Defines the jackboot under that affable decorum.
Let it not be forgotten that this summer the Teagues * in Belfast,
out of the body's agony, made the world their forum.

(*All Things Counter*, 1986)

---

* Teagues: derisive epithet used to denote a Catholic in Northern
Ireland; from Tadhg, the Irish for Timothy – "Tim".

The Department Regrets

Papal Visit, October 1979

Certainly our record is not bad as President Bokassas
Who killed (or ate) one hundred children.
So far none of ours have died on O'Connell Bridge
Where they squat nightly, frozen, wind-ridden.

The rain lashes through the balustrades
Rattling the pitiful trays, but having no effect
On that weird smile fixed on their faces
Which their vacant eyes do not reflect.

Then this week the Pope came
And truly a miracle took place.
The children vanished from O'Connell Bridge,
It was all part of a new face.

Created by our concerned Rulers,
Concerned that His Holiness might see
How we Christians love one another
Beyond the boundaries of the Holy See.

The pious nod and say
It wouldn't be that way
Unless there was a reason in it,
God disposes every minute.

It's hard to believe what a shower we are
To actually blame this on God.
Trust us not to call a spade a spade
When we can call it a flowering rod.

(*All Things Counter*, 1986)

Words Alone Are Certain Good

It's great to put a word to work
That has fallen out of fashion,
One that other writers shirk
Unused, abused and just forgotten.

Fit it in a poem and then
Have it glow as was intended.
So poor word is fine again
Back in business feeling splendid.

(2002)

Sisyphus Wins

Call no man happy who is not dead
But of this one it must be said;
Though he's in a wheelchair and paralysed
His condition is not easily analysed.
He drives on the road instead of the pavement,
A guy who believes in freedom of movement,
He can even get quite melodramatic
And turn and charge oncoming traffic.
Arms whirling he swerves in and out
Destabilising them with an almighty shout.
When he rolls out as his dash is completed
He's covered in dust and overheated,
But his face transformed, gleams in glory
He's learned a way to tell his story
Found his space by avoiding the pavement
Not giving a fiddlers what the gods meant
And leaves them now without a function
Himself in command at the next junction.

(1999)

NOTE: The Gods punished Sisyphus by making him push a
huge rock up a mountain. As soon as he reached the sum-
mit, the weight of the stone would force him to let it go, and
roll back down again so that he would have to begin his task
once again.

Scared

A tawny haired tinker girl
As I passed showed me a blue eye
There was a welcome in her brown face
If I stopped by.

That her man might be skittering near,
By heavens I knew
Skinning rabbits and poaching fish
And he'd skin me too.

Then she'd throw back her lovely head
And laugh at the beating I'd get
I tell you that's why I shirked
The blue eye that beckons me yet.

(*Lifestyles*, 1973)

from "Galerias"

after Antonio Machado

Calling to my heart, one fine day,
With the scent of jasmin, the wind spoke.

"In exchange for this perfume
I ask only the perfume of your roses."

"I have no roses. There are no
Flowers in my garden. Only the dead."

"I will banish the moaning of fountains,
The dying leaves and the stricken petals."
Then the wind vanished, leaving my heart bleeding –
"Soul what have you done with your sad garden."

Translated by Ulick O'Connor
(*All Things Counter*, 1986)

Song of the Flame of Living Love

After St. John of the Cross

Oh flame of the living love
That gently makes its wound
In my soul's core, oh pulse that's beating
Since I've never found you proud,
Be pleased to leave me now
And break the thread of this delicious meeting.

Oh soothing cautery,
Oh wound most delicate,
Oh gentle touch; oh caress that's thrilling,
Foretaste of eternity,
Which cancels every debt,
Thou dost restore to life by sweetly killing.

Oh burning lantern's crest
In whose reflection bright
The obscure caverns of the senses open.
Once dark, the lover's breast
Fills with colour and with light
And exquisite sensations are awoken.

How lovingly and gently
Memory murmurs in my breast
Where secretly alone you have been moving.
Breathing there most sweetly,
Full of goodness and at rest,
How courteously you lure me to this loving.

Translated by Ulick O'Connor
(*All Things Counter*, 1986)

Homage to Philip Larkin

A lot would love to have had Larkin's know-how,
To hold on to three birds at the one time.
Each one thinking she was numero uno
Not just a player in a lover's mime.

Larkin's dad had the same pot-luck
A master when it came to shifting the onus,
Though the son said your parents "fuck you up",
It was from Dad he learned to strike a bonus.

Both had the mandarin touch, to balance
Like a ball on the squirt of a fountain.
Good bookeeping was the best insurance,
If it came to a dodgy countdown.

We make a hero of the crafty Greek
Who ensured misfortune missed him.
Why not points for Phil and Syd
Who steered their schooners through the system.

(2003)

NOTE: Philip Larkin (as well as keeping three mistresses)
built up Hull University Library to be one of the best modern
ones in Britain while Sydney Larkin, his father, treasurer of
Coventry City was also much admired for foresight and
achievement. Before the War, Larkin senior had shown himself
not unsympathetic to the Right, and had a statue of Hitler on
his desk, which at the touch of a button jumped to the salute.

Green Devil

Jealousy that's what
Can have you crouched up a tree
Squinting to see
Who's giving her what's what

Jealousy is when bank accounts
Don't count or the cancer word
When you're never bored
And only one thing counts

Who is the other hack?
Is she over the limit?
And though you won't admit it
Can you get her back.

(1985)

Lament for Naoise

from Deirdre,
A play in the Noh form performed at the Abbey Theatre in 1986

The ancient tale of Deirdre tells how she was reared as an orphan by King Conor of Ulster. He wanted to marry her but she ran away to Scotland with Naoise, the greatest warrior in his army, and his brothers Ardan and Ainle. King Conor lured Naoise and his brothers and Deirdre back to Ulster through a trick and then had them slaughtered by his army. He married Deirdre but she thwarted him by killing herself with a knife.

In the Noh form we are introduced to a figure on the wheel of reincarnation cleansing themselves of some sin in a series of rebirths until they reach *satori* or enlightenment. In my version I suggested that Deirdre had a premonition of Conor's intention, but rather than leave Naoise went with him to their death.

SCHOLAR But you died rather than leave Naoise.

DEIRDRE I drove Naoise back to Conor.
              I knew when Fergus McRoy came
              To ask them to leave Scotland
              And return to the Royal Court
              That Naoise would be killed.
              I knew that old Fox-King
              Who reared me for the lust of his age
              too well for that. I knew his tricks
              But my fear was that one day Naoise would leave me.
              He would see I had torn him from the soil
              He grew in. He would have gone with his brothers
              To other battles. Soldiering was his trade.

One day he would not return.
If he was slain by the armies of Conor
At least I would be at his side.
I urged him back to treachery
Rather than die without him... ... ...
Naoise, with the deep sound of the waves in your voice
Ainle with the fresh cry of the thrush
Ardan that had the note of the horn in his throat.
Naoise, dear the grey eye that women loved
Fierce when the enemy came it grew
When he rambled in the woods
Delightful was his cry through the dark forest.
Dear to Conor was the sound of pipers
Sweeter to me the cry of Naoise over the fields
I cannot sleep. I put no purple on my nails.

(*Three Noh Plays*, 1980)

Easter Week 1986

I

Seventy years ago this morn
Our great poet said
A terrible beauty was born
But is it now dead?
No trumpet call
Or Cabinet to mourn [1]
In memory of your deed
At Kilmainham wall
Or was it still born?
Just a dream
Scorned in our waking hours,
That proved in the cold light
Beyond our powers.
Have we paid the price
For your sacrifice?

II

Awake now for seventy years
Long lines of the hopeless file.
Yes: they are kept alive
In approved imperial style.

III

Though we have conquered in our own way
Using another tongue to spell
That our empire is of the word
And can dominate as well

As Roman wall or Norman tower,
We are still living in pawn.
Divided, exhausted, confused spectators
Of an uneasy dawn,
While police fire above the head
Of crowds, for imagined slights,
Their backs turned on that sacrificial shed.
How long before they lower their sights? [2]

(All Things Counter, 1986)

NOTES:

[1] There was no official commemoration of the 70th anniversary of the Easter Rising in 1986.

[2] Gardai at the GPO that Easter fired over the heads of unarmed demonstrators.

Ed è subito sera

From the Italian of Salvatore Quasimodo,
Nobel Prizewinner 1959

Alone in the earth's heart each stands bare,
Pierced by an arrow of the sun:
Suddenly, evening's there.

Eighteen poems by Charles Baudelaire

from *Les Fleurs du Mal*

translated by Ulick O'Connor

When the First section of *Les Fleurs Du Mal* appeared
in a volume of eighteen poems in 1857. Baudelaire
was prosecuted for a breach of public morality. Among
those poems censored were two which are included
here, *Femmes Damnées* and *Lethe*. The ban on the
censored poems was not lifted until 31st May, 1949.

(*Poems of the Damned*, 1995)

The Giantess

In that age when nature with her powerful pulse
Would each day some prodigious child bear fruit,
I would have loved to have lived close to a young giantess,
Like a voluptuous cat lying at a queen's foot.

I would have watched her body flower like her soul,
Expanding famously at her mighty game;
And from the mists which round her eyes would swirl,
Muse, if her heart nourished some tragic flame:

To explore those splendid contours at my ease;
Negotiate the slopes of those enormous knees;
And in the summer, when the malign sun would keep

Her stretched across the fields prone in heat,
In the shadow of her breasts nonchalantly to sleep,
Like a peaceful hamlet at the mountain's feet.

Glad To Be Dead

Deep in slimy earth surrounded by snails
I want to dig myself a gaping pit,
Where like a shark in a wave, snug beyond gales
I can stretch my creaking bones a little bit.

I hate tombs, legacies, those sort of shows
Rather than ask for some sign of remorse
By staying alive, I would prefer to ask the crows
To lap the blood from my loathsome corpse.

Worms without ears or eyes, to your dark company
Admit now a new friend, joyous and free
As for you prosperous philosophers, sons of filth,

Across my tomb step without remorse or dread,
Let me know if you find some new torment built
For this dogsbody without soul among the dead.

Sorrows of the Moon

How lazily to-night the moon dreams above the land;
Like a rare beauty on her cushioned couch,
Who before she slips to sleep allows her hand
Caress her breast, with slight and sensuous touch.

On the satined back of soft drifts of foam
Swooning, she reclines, as night flies by,
Lifting her eyes towards those shapes that roam
Like flowers, the floating terraces of the sky.

When sometimes the languid one lets fall
On earth just one furtive tear, that's all,
A pious poet, disdainful of sleep's prize,

Will cradle that pale tear within his hand
With its reflecting irises like a diamond band
To treasure in his heart, far from the sun's eyes.

The Rebel

The Angel swoops like an eagle from the firmament,
Grabs the miscreant's hair in his strong fist
And shaking it says 'There is just one Commandment.
(See here I am your good Angel) I must insist!

'You'll learn to love with no hint of distaste,
The poor, wicked, the stupid, that whole dazed forum,
So that for Jesus, when He comes, you will have placed
The triumphant carpet of your love before Him.

'This is charity. Before your heart grows cold,
Rekindle your ecstasy within His fold,
That true voluptuousness whose charm won't fade away.'

The Angel chastising, as he would (indeed) love
The blasphemer, pummels him with giant fists from above;
But the damned one answers always 'I will not obey.'

The Cat

Within my head there perambulates,
As if in his own apartment,
This gorgeous cat, strong and with refinement,
You scarcely hear his purr as it vibrates.

The tone is so tender so laid back,
Whether his voice soothes or scolds,
With resonance and depth it rolls
This is his secret, his real knack.

This voice, which pearls and flows
To the dark corners of my mind,
Pulses in me like a poem, I find
I'm spellbound, my being glows.

His sound can calm the most cruel hurt
Imbued with such soothing prescience.
It can suggest the longest sentence
Without ever having to use a word.

There is no bow which can wing
My heart, that most perfect instrument,
And have it quiver with such sentiment,
It rings like music on a throbbing string,

As your voice, mysterious cat,
Which is like that of an angel
In which harmony and sweetness mingle
Exotic, seraphic, yes. I may call you that.

From his fur, white and russet-brown,
Proceeds so sweet a perfume
That from his kiss alone I almost swoon,
Just one caress and I am undone.

He is the real owner of this pad,
He judges, he presides, to inspire
Everything here as his own empire,
Surely he is some spirit or a god.

When my eyes are drawn to this feline elf
As they would be to a lover,
He returns my gaze, careless what I discover
And what do I find there, I find myself.

I gaze with wonder and my caution shrinks
Under the fire of those pale pupils,
Those clear lanterns and twilight jewels
That contemplate me firmly without a blink.

Don Juan In Hell

(after 'The Impenitent' by Delacroix)

When Don Juan descended to the stream below
He first of all to Charon paid his fees,
A swarthy beggar took the oars to row
With cruel and powerful arms, proud as Antisthenes.

Dishevelled gowns displaying their drooping breasts,
Women writhing under a tumultuous sky
Like a great herd of sacrificial beasts,
Trail behind him with a continual cry.

Laughing Sganarelle comes to claim his wages,
While Don Luis with quavering hand declares
To all the dead who gather at these edges,
This is the blackguard son who mocked his silver hairs.

The chaste Elvira shivering and thin, meanwhile
Faces the treacherous spouse she once adored,
To win from him just one last supreme smile
Such as lit his face when first he pledged his word.

Cased in armour, a huge stone man on board,
Seizes the helm and navigates the Sound.
But our cool hero, leaning upon his sword,
Watches only the wake's foam, scorning to look around.

The Albatross

Often to amuse themselves, the sailors catch
The albatross, giant creatures of the sky,
Indolent companions of the voyage who watch
The white ships on the bitter foam glide by.

Hardly have they hauled their captive through the rail
Than these sky-kings, clumsy now and shamed,
Begin to let their great wings droop and trail
Like oars beside them, pitiably tamed.

Winged voyager, how feeble you've become,
Lately so lovely, ugly once on board.
With his pipe a sailor goads the beak that's dumb;
Another limping, mocks the cripple who once soared.

The poet resembles these princes of the clouds,
Daring the tempest and the hunter's slings.
Exiled on earth amid the jeers of crowds,
His movement impeded by his giant wings.

Icarus' Lament

The lovers of prostitutes
Are satisfied, awoken.
Look at me, arms broken
Hugging clouds as substitutes.

Those fantastic stars, the ones
Which blaze from the skies' depth,
Have blinded me till I am left
With only memories of suns.

I've tried to estimate
In space, where end and centre lie.
Beneath an unknown burning eye
My wings melt and disintegrate.

Burned by the beauty I crave,
I don't have the sublime bliss
Of putting my name on that abyss,
Which will serve as my grave.

Little Old Ladies (III)

Little old ladies, how often have I followed them!
Especially one who, as the dying sun departs
And vermilion wounds bloody the evening's rim,
Would sit on a park bench, pensive and apart,

Delighting in those concerts with their ringing brass
With which the army sometimes grace our parks,
Making us feel reborn as the golden evening pass
And some heroism pours into people's hearts.

Her, I recall still, proud, with a queen's stance,
Absorbed in the valour of some martial quarrel.
Sometimes her eye would open with an eagle glance,
The marble forehead lifted for the laurel.

The End of the Day

Beneath a thin sun
Life writhes without reason
Moves shamelessly, runs,
Till on the horizon

Comes sensuous night,
And as hunger eases
Shame takes its flight,
The poet says 'Oh Jesus

My spirits oppress me,
My back cries for respite,
Though dark dreams enmesh me

I will roll with delight
In the curtains of night,
Whose shades will refresh me.'

The Ransom

Man, to pay his ransom,
Has two rich fields of soil
Where he must plough and toil
With the blade of reason.

For the smallest rose to grow,
To extract some ears of corn,
The water must be drawn
From the sweat of his grey brow.

One is Art, the other Love,
Which the Judge will adjudicate
On that awful day of fate
When he will arrive from above.

There must be at his disposal
Full barns and luscious flowers
Whose colours and contours
Will win the Angels' approval.

The Enemy

My youth was nothing but a darkening storm
Enlivened now and then by brilliant suns;
But rain and thunder shaped a different form
And few fresh flowers survive the withered ones.

Now that I have reached the autumn of the mind,
I must find work for every rake and spade
To clear the flooded land and leave behind
New pastures, where tomb-like pits are laid.

Who knows if the flowers of which I dream
Will find fresh soil on this new shore swept clean,
Some mystic power, from which another life can start.

Ah, the pity of it; time diverts life's flood
And that secret enemy which devours the heart
Sustains itself upon our bartered blood.

Lethe

Rest on my heart, cruel and sullen one.
Adored tigress, monster of indolent air,
I long in the thickness of your tawny hair,
To plunge my trembling fingers till I'm done.

To bury the burden of my aching head
In the perfume of your towering skirts,
Like a withered flower, to savour though it hurts
The sweet odour of a love that's dead.

Rather than live, for sleep my body longs
To slip into a slumber sweet as death.
I shower remorselessly kisses with each breath
Upon your body with its gleam of bronze.

Nothing can equal your bed's abyss
To engulf and soothe my bitter cries,
On those lips deep oblivion lies,
And all Lethe surges through your kiss.

From now on I shall act as Fate requires,
And use the unhappiness from which it stemmed,
A willing martyr and innocent condemned,
Who fuels his agony with his own desires.

I shall drink to drown my rancour for a start,
Nectar, sweet hemlock and the rest
From the ravishing tips of your erect breast
Which never once has held a captive heart.

The Passerby

My ears deafened in the street's mayhem:
A woman in full mourning passes by
Majestic, sad, a languid hand held high,
Lifting and balancing the borders of her hem.

Noble, statuesque in limb, you sense her power;
My mind on fire I see behind her eye
Some tempest trembling in a livid sky,
Softnesses which bewitch, pleasures which devour.

A flash of lightning – night – beauty fled
In whose glance I have been suddenly reborn
Shall I see you in another world instead?

Elsewhere; perhaps never; condemned to mourn
I know not where you fled – or you not where I go
You whom I could have loved – you who knew it so.

The Wine of Lovers

What a space we have today;
No bridle, bit or spur to stay
Our rapture; as we roam the sky
Wine as our horse, you and I.

Like two reckless angels driven
By a fevered sea towards heaven,
In the crystal blue of morning
Follow the mirage that's forming.

Balanced gently on the wings
Of friendly whirlwinds let us glide,
Share the delirium that it brings.

My sister, swimming side by side,
We'll skim the surface till it seems
We've reached the Eden of my dreams.

Meditation

Oh sorrow mine, be wise and unafraid
You longed for evening; see it falls out there
The fading light softening the city's shade,
Bringing peace to some and to others care.

While that vile crew, driven by Pleasure's whip
The cruel torturer, must reap remorse
In slavish feasts; oh Sorrow mine, slip
Your hand in mine; and seek some other source

Far from here. See in torn robes the lost years
Lean from the skies' balconies while Regret appears
Smiling from the waves, as evening pales.

The dying sun slips down beneath an arch
And from the Eastern sky a long shroud trails.
Hold, beloved, hold, sweet Night is on the march.

The Damned Women
(Delphine and Hippolyte)

In the white clearness of the lamp's last hiss,
On cushions soaked in scent with beating heart,
Hippolyte dreamed of that tremendous kiss
Which tore the veil of her innocence apart.

She searches now with tempest troubled eyes
The receding sky of the simplicity she'd lost,
Like a traveller who turns his head and sighs
For blue horizons, which that morning he had crossed.

Her tired eyes, her languid tears, her frown
And dazed air, superb voluptuousness,
Her limp arms thrown like futile weapons down,
Served only to enhance her frail loveliness.

Stretched at her feet, contented now and gay,
Delphine devours her with shining eyes;
Like a savage beast who contemplates its prey,
Having with its teeth, first marked the prize.

Strong beauty, before frail beauty superbly kneels,
Breathing sensuously the wine of victory,
Leaning towards her love, she hopes to win
Some sweet token of their ecstasy.

Delphine seeks in her pale victim's eye
The silent hymn aroused on pleasure's fields,
Which flutters the eyelids after a prolonged sigh
In sublime thanksgiving for the gift she yields.

'Hippolyte, dear heart, can I now assume
That you will not submit in any way,
The sacred sacrifice of your first roses' bloom
To violent gusts, which will wither them away.

'My kisses are just like flies that flit
And caress at evening the glass face of lakes;
Not those of one who'd carve a cruel rut
Like the furrow which the brutal ploughshare makes;

'Man will trample you like a savage herd
Of horse or cattle with pitiless hooves,
Hippolyte, my sister, can you not speak one word;
My soul, my heart my half of me, all that I choose.

'Grant from blue eyes glowing like stars at night;
Just one bewitching look that you may send,
And I shall lift the veil on still more rare delights,
Lull you to sleep in dreams that have no end!'

Hippolyte now raised her young head from the shade.
'Call me not ungrateful, nor do I regret in the least
What we have done my Delphine; but I am troubled
     and afraid
As if it was the night after some fearful feast.

'Swooping down on me I feel a frightful load;
Black ranks marching, a host of phantoms without shape
Trying to lure me, along a shifting road
Towards a bleeding sky from which there's no escape.

'Have we then committed some dreadful sin
How else explain this terror which endures
When you say "My Angel!" I tremble within
Yet my lips are relentlessly drawn to yours.

'Don't look at me like that, sister of my choice;
You whom I love forever and for whom,
Even if you've set a snare, I still rejoice,
Though it may be the commencement of my doom.'

Delphine, tossing her tragic mane,
And like a goddess from her plinth above,
Trembling in prophecy, makes her daring claim;
'Who speaks of hell before the power of love?

'A curse on that useless dreamer who first thought,
When faced with love's inexplicable laws,
That he could solve the mystery if he sought
To mix some honour with its anarchic cause.

'Who seeks to unify in mystic kin
Shade and light, day with the night above,
Will never warm his paralytic skin
With that scarlet sun, we give the name of Love!

'Go find some stupid oaf among the pack;
Deliver your virgin heart to his cruel clutch;
Then pale with horror and remorse come back
And show me your breasts savaged by his touch.

'One can only serve one master of the heart,'
But the girl burst out in a sudden shriek of pain;
'I feel as if I am being ripped apart,
Some gaping abyss where love once has lain.

'Burning like a volcano nothing can withstand
This groaning monster, whose will must have its way
Or quench the Fury's thirst, waving in her hand
A flaming torch to burn my blood away.

'Since between the world and us a curtain must exist,
In that langour, which will penetrate this room
I annihilate myself upon these breasts
And there discover the freshness of the tomb!'

Descend unhappy victims and begin
That infernal voyage, where you will be hurled
Into the deepest pit, and all your sins
Scourged by a wind which is not of this world.

Far from the living and condemned to roam
You race like wolves across the desert shelf;
Disordered souls, seeking a fate that is your own,
While ignoring the divinity within yourself!

The Owls

Black yews shelter them as they wait
Owls perched aloft in regular rows.
Like strange gods they view the world below,
Red eyes flashing, and meditate.

Motionless they occupy this space,
Until that melancholy hour will come,
When thrusting down the sliding sun
The shadows will resume their regular place.

From such the wise become aware
That if we don't accept things as they are,
Shun the tumult and the movement,

Obsessed with what is and what is not;
We must shoulder our own punishment
For having wished to change our lot.

About the Author

Among ULICK O'CONNOR's prodigious literary output as biographer, playwright, literary historian and critic, he is of course a poet. Since his first book of poems *Life Styles* appeared in 1973 he has been writing and publishing, albeit intermittently, memorable poetry for more than four decades. His engagement with his subject matter, his deft use of form, craft and above all lyricism, define these poems and make it a pleasure to rediscover them or encounter them for a first time. In a judicious selection, they are gathered here along with his translations from numerous languages, including his exceptional renderings of Baudelaire and more recent poems that have appeared in journals over the past decade.

Ulick O'Connor's first book of poems *Life Styles* was published by Hamish Hamilton and Dolmen Press in 1975. He went on to write five others among them *All Things Counter* (1986), and *One is Animate* (1990). His translations of Baudelaire were published by Wolfhound Press in 1995. It received an outstanding reception and Michel Déon of Académie Francaise wrote in introducing it,

'The poem is reborn before our very eyes and is music to our ears, not translated but recreated. I am rendered speechless. The poet O'Connor offers to the poet Baudelaire an unparalleled "treasure"'.

Ulick O'Connor is also noted for his verse plays in the Noh form. He was guest of the Japanese Government in 1995 when he went out to work with the Japanese National Theatre. His best known work in this form *Deirdre* was revived this year and played alongside Yeats 'Deirdre' in the National Library celebrations of the poet's work.

Ulick O'Connor's books include biographies of Oliver St. Gogarty, Brendan Behan and the highly successful *Celtic Dawn*, a portrait of the Irish Literary Renaissance. *The Ulick O'Connor Diaries* published in 2001 by John Murray London were much praised by English critics, the Times (London) comparing him to Boswell. His successes as a playwright include *Execution* described by the Evening Standard as "dynamite"; *Joyicity* by the New York Times as "supreme", and his duo about Oscar Wilde, *A Trinity of Two* as "elegant, probing and beautiful" (The Stage).